A CENTURY OF

PIANO · VOCAL · GUITAR

Broadway

1900 - 1999

ISBN 0-634-00979-6

HAL•LEONARD®
CORPORATION

7777 W. BLUEMOUND RD. P.O. BOX 13819 MILWAUKEE, WI 53213

Visit Hal Leonard Online at
www.halleonard.com

CONTENTS
Chronological Listing

CONTENTS
Alphabetical Listing

Tell Me Pretty Maiden
FLORODORA
1900

Words by OWEN HALL
Music by LESLIE STUART

must love some one, real - ly And it might as well be you!

must love some one, real - ly And it might as well be you!

In the Good Old Summertime

THE DEFENDER
1901

Words by REN SHIELDS
Music by GEORGE EVANS

Moderately

There's a time in each
To swim in the

year, that we al-ways hold dear, good old
pool, you'd play "hook-y" from school, good old

sum-mer time;_____ with the birds and the trees-es and
sum-mer time;_____ you'd play "ring-a-ros-ie" with

UNDER THE BAMBOO TREE
SALLY IN OUR ALLEY
1902

Words and Music by ROBERT COLE
and J. ROSAMOND JOHNSON

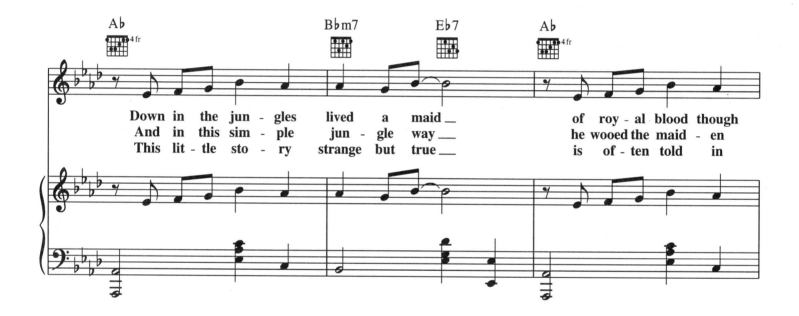

Down in the jun - gles lived a maid ___ of roy - al blood though
And in this sim - ple jun - gle way ___ he wooed the maid - en
This lit - tle sto - ry strange but true ___ is of - ten told in

dus - ky shade, ___ a marked im - pres - sion once she made ___
ev' - ry day, ___ by sing - ing what he once had to say. ___
Ma - ta - boo ___ of how this Zu - lu tried to woo ___

I Can't Do the Sum

BABES IN TOYLAND
1903

Words by GLEN McDONOUGH
Music by VICTOR HERBERT

mates were al - most six feet high, And the bos' - n near the same, Would
quite for - got the steer - ing gear, On her hon - eyed lips to sup, How
bill of fare were thir-teen nine - ty five, And poor Har - old had but four, How
naught but sun - ny out - side rooms, In a neigh - bor - hood of tone, How
if with ev - 'ry pound of tea, He will give two cut glass plates, How

you sub - tract or mul - ti - ply, To find the cap - tain's name?
soon could twen - ty men with brooms, Sweep Clare and Gwen - nie up?
ma - ny things would Har - old strike, Be - fore he struck the floor?
old would those ten chil - dren be, Be - fore they found a home?
soon would Wil - lie break his face, On his new roll - er skates?

8va

(rhythmically writes on slate)

Put down six and car - ry two,

(on slate)

Gee! but this is hard to do;

You can think and think and think Till your brains are

(on slate)

numb, I don't care what teach - er says,

1
I can't do the sum.

2
sum.

Give My Regards to Broadway

LITTLE JOHNNY JONES
1904

Words and Music by
GEORGE M. COHAN

Kiss Me Again

MLLE. MODISTE
1905

Fifi.

Words by HENRY BLOSSOM
Music by VICTOR HERBERT

Ah! _____ with lords and la - dies great to kneel and kiss my hand. A king up - on the throne To woo me for his own, Ah! the _ fair - est ev - er seen. Ah! _____ Ah! _____ Ah! _____ Ah! _ who would not be queen.

Valse lente.

Sweet sum-mer breeze, whis-per-ing trees, Stars shin-ing soft-ly a-bove;_____ Ros-es in bloom, waft-ed per-fume, Sleep-y birds dream-ing of love._____ Safe in your arms, far from a-larms,

Mary's a Grand Old Name
FORTY-FIVE MINUTES FROM BROADWAY
1906

Words and Music by
GEORGE M. COHAN

My moth-er's name was Ma - ry, she was so good and
Now, when her name is Ma - ry, there is no false-ness

true; ___ Be - cause her name was Ma - ry,
there; ___ When to Ma - rie she'll va - ry,

she called me Ma - ry, too. ___ She was - n't gay or
she'll sure - ly bleach her hair. ___ Though Ma - ry's or - di -

air - y, but plain as she could be; ___
na - ry, Ma - rie is fair to see; ___

I hate to meet a fair - y who calls her-self Ma - rie. ___
Don't ev - er fear sweet Ma - ry, be-ware of sweet Ma - rie. ___

CHORUS Slowly

For it is Ma - ry, Ma - ry, plain as a - ny name can

36

The Merry Widow Waltz
The Merry Widow
1907

Words by ADRIAN ROSS
Music by FRANZ LEHAR

Gold - en glow - ing lamps are

Cuddle Up a Little Closer, Lovey Mine

THE THREE TWINS
1908

Words by OTTO HARBACH
Music by KARL HOSCHNA

Falling in Love
THE CHOCOLATE SOLDIER
1909

Lyrics by STANISLAUS STANGE
Music by OSCAR STRAUS

Andante

ALEXIUS:

Oh

when   you ___ smile   and feel like   cry - ing,   and when you
when   at   night   you should be   sleep - ing,   you rest - less

poco rall.

tranquillo

can - not tell the rea - son   why, _____   You're in
lie   and toss a - bout   the   bed, _____   You're in

love   when you smile   while you are   cry - ing,   Or when you
love   when you watch   the shad - ows   creep - ing,   Or when at

AH! SWEET MYSTERY OF LIFE
NAUGHTY MARIETTA
1910

Music by VICTOR HERBERT
Lyrics by RIDA JOHNSON YOUNG

WOODMAN, WOODMAN, SPARE THAT TREE!

ZIEGFELD FOLLIES
1911

Words and Music by IRVING BERLIN
and VINCENT BRYAN

56

Giannina Mia
THE FIREFLY
1912

Words by OTTO HARBACH
Music by RUDOLF FRIML

SWEETHEARTS
SWEETHEARTS
1913

Words by ROBERT B. SMITH
Music by VICTOR HERBERT

If you ask where love is found, the sort of love that's fond _ and _ true, I will bid you look a-round; it may be ver-y near _ to _ you.

Some-times love is ver-y try-ing, but you real-ly must not mind it; If it comes not to your sigh-ing,

They Didn't Believe Me

THE GIRL FROM UTAH
1914

Words by HERBERT REYNOLDS
Music by JEROME KERN

68

I Love a Piano
STOP! LOOK! LISTEN!
1915

Words and Music by
IRVING BERLIN

Where Did Robinson Crusoe Go with Friday on Saturday Night?

ROBINSON CRUSOE, JR.
1916

Words by SAM M. LEWIS and JOE YOUNG
Music by GEO. W. MEYER

78

CLEOPATTERER
LEAVE IT TO JANE
1917

Words and Music by JEROME KERN
and P.G. WODEHOUSE

In days of old be - side the Nile A
And when she tired as girls will do, Of
She danced new danc - es now and then Of The

fam - ous Queen there dwelt; Her clothes were few, but
Bill or Jack or Jim, The time had she did them,
sort that make you blush. Each time she come, his

full of style; Her fig - ure slim and svelt; On
friends all knew, To say good - bye to him. She
scores of men Got in - jured in the rush. They'd

Rock-A-Bye Your Baby with a Dixie Melody

SINBAD
1918

Words by SAM M. LEWIS and JOE YOUNG
Music by JEAN SCHWARTZ

A Pretty Girl Is Like a Melody
ZIEGFELD FOLLIES
1919

Words and Music by
IRVING BERLIN

I have an ear for mu-sic, and I have an eye for a maid. _____ I like a pret-ty girl-ie, with each pret-ty tune that's played. _____ They go to-geth-er,

LOOK FOR THE SILVER LINING
SALLY
1920

Words by BUDDY DeSYLVA
Music by JEROME KERN

Eb   Bb   Cm   Gm   Fm   Eb   Fm   Bb7

I am sure your point of view will ease the dai - ly grind,

Eb   F7   Bb7   Eb   Bb7

So I'll keep re - peat-ing in my mind. _____

Refrain *(slowly, with warm expression)*

Eb   Bb7   Eb

Look for _____ the sil - ver lin - ing _____

p

molto legato

Ab

_____ When - e'er a cloud ap - pears in the

My Man
(Mon Homme)
ZIEGFELD FOLLIES
1921

Words by ALBERT WILLEMETZ
and JACQUES CHARLES
English Words by CHANNING POLLOCK
Music by MAURICE YVAIN

It's cost me a lot, but there's one thing that I've got it's my man,__
Some-times I say if I just could get a-way with my man,__
Sur cet-te terr', ma seul' joie, mon seul bon-heur C'est mon hom-me

cold and wet, tired you bet, but all that I soon for-get with my man.__
he'd go straight sure as fate, for it nev-er is too late for my man.__
J'ai don-né tout c'que j'ai, mon a-mour et tout mon cœur, A mon hom-me,

He's not much for looks, and no he-ro out of books is my man.__
I just like to dream of a cot-tage by a stream with my man,__
Et mé-me la nuit Quand je ré-ve, c'est de lui De mon hom-me.

I'LL BUILD A STAIRWAY TO PARADISE

GEORGE WHITE'S SCANDALS
1922

Words by B.G. DeSYLVA
and IRA GERSHWIN
Music by GEORGE GERSHWIN

The Waltz of Long Ago
Music Box Revue
1923

Words and Music by
IRVING BERLIN

Moderate Waltz

Jazz danc - ing now - a - days does not ap - peal to me.

INDIAN LOVE CALL
ROSE-MARIE
1924

Lyrics by OTTO HARBACH and OSCAR HAMMERSTEIN II
Music by RUDOLF FRIML

Manhattan
THE GARRICK GAIETIES
1925

Words by LORENZ HART
Music by RICHARD RODGERS

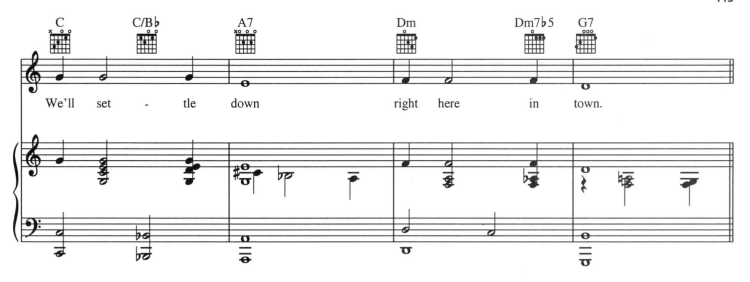

We'll set - tle down right here in town.

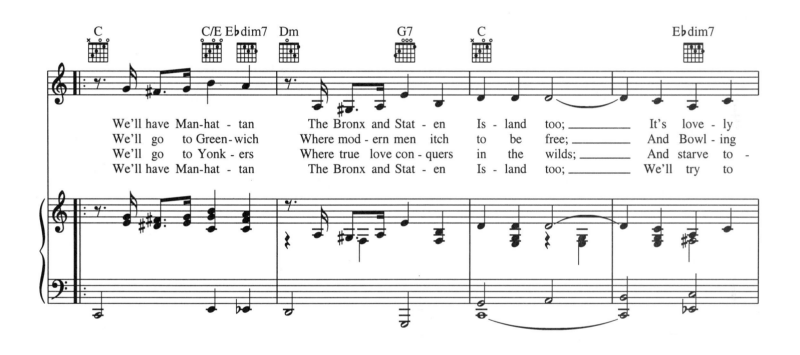

We'll have Man-hat - tan The Bronx and Stat - en Is - land too; _____ It's love - ly
We'll go to Green-wich Where mod - ern men itch to be free; _____ And Bowl - ing
We'll go to Yonk - ers Where true love con - quers in the wilds; _____ And starve to -
We'll have Man-hat - tan The Bronx and Stat - en Is - land too; _____ We'll try to

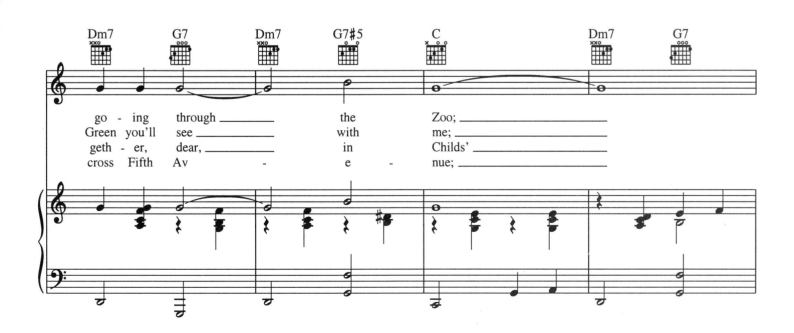

go - ing through _____ the Zoo; _____
Green you'll see _____ with me; _____
geth - er, dear, _____ in Childs' _____
cross Fifth Av - e - nue; _____

The Birth of the Blues
GEORGE WHITE'S SCANDALS OF 1926
1926

Words by B.G. DeSYLVA and LEW BROWN
Music by RAY HENDERSON

BILL
SHOW BOAT
1927

Lyrics by P.G. WODEHOUSE and OSCAR HAMMERSTEIN II
Music by JEROME KERN

JULIE:

I used to dream that I would dis-
golf or ten-nis or

cov - er_____ the per - fect lov - er some day. I know I'd re-cog-
po - lo,_____ or sing a so - lo, or row. He is - n't half as

nize him if ev - er he came round my
hand - some as doz - ens of men that I

122

Makin' Whoopee!
WHOOPEE!
1928

Lyrics by GUS KAHN
Music by WALTER DONALDSON

With a Song in My Heart
SPRING IS HERE
1929

Words by LORENZ HART
Music by RICHARD RODGERS

Moderately

Stacy: Though I know that we meet ev-'ry night And we
Betty: Oh, the moon's not a moon for a night; And these

could - n't have changed since the last time, To my joy and de - light it's a
stars will not twin - kle and fade out! And the words in my ears will re -

new kind of love at first sight. _____ Though it's you and it's I all the
sound for the rest of my years. _____ In the morn - ing I'll find with de -

Ten Cents a Dance
SIMPLE SIMON
1930

Words by LORENZ HART
Music by RICHARD RODGERS

know, One that the pal- ace fea- tures At ex- act- ly a dime a

throw.

(slowly, quasi rubato)

Ten cents a dance; That's what they pay me.

Gosh, how they weigh me down! Ten cents a dance, Pan- sies and rough guys,

Tough guys who tear my gown! Sev- en to mid- night, I hear drums,

LIFE IS JUST A BOWL OF CHERRIES

GEORGE WHITE'S SCANDALS (1931 EDITION)
1931

Words and Music by LEW BROWN
and RAY HENDERSON

LET'S HAVE ANOTHER
CUP O' COFFEE
FACE THE MUSIC
1932

Words and Music by
IRVING BERLIN

SMOKE GETS IN YOUR EYES

ROBERTA
1933

Words by OTTO HARBACH
Music by JEROME KERN

They asked me how I knew my true love was true. _____ I of course re- plied, some-thing here in-side, can-not be de-

You're a Builder Upper

LIFE BEGINS AT 8:40
1934

Lyric by IRA GERSHWIN and E.Y. HARBURG
Music by HAROLD ARLEN

Moderately

When you want to, you are a - ble to make me feel that

I'm Clark Ga - ble; then, next min - ute, you make me feel I'm

some - thing from the Zoo. First you warm up

150

LITTLE GIRL BLUE
JUMBO
1935

Words by LORENZ HART
Music by RICHARD RODGERS

Sit there and count your fin-gers, what can you do? Old girl, you're

through. Sit there and count your lit-tle fin-gers, Un-

153

I Can't Get Started with You

ZIEGFELD FOLLIES
1936

Words by IRA GERSHWIN
Music by VERNON DUKE

MY FUNNY VALENTINE
BABES IN ARMS
1937

Words by LORENZ HART
Music by RICHARD RODGERS

made, Thy va - cant brow and thy tous - led hair con -

ceal thy good in - tent. Thou no - ble, up - right,

truth - ful, sin - cere and slight - ly dop - ey gent, you're

My fun - ny Val - en - tine, Sweet com - ic

164

My Heart Belongs to Daddy
LEAVE IT TO ME
1938

Words and Music by
COLE PORTER

I used to fall ___ In love with all ___ Those boys who maul ___ The young cut-ies. ___ But now I find ___ I'm more in-clined ___

But in the Morning, No
DUBARRY WAS A LADY
1939

Words and Music by
COLE PORTER

BUT IN THE MORNING, NO

REFRAIN 2

He: Do you like the mountains, dear?
　　Kindly tell me, if so.
She: Yes, I like the mountains, dear,
　　But in the morning, no
He: Are you good at climbing, dear?
　　Kindly tell me, if so.
She: Yes, I'm good at climbing, dear,
　　But in the morning, no.
　　When the light of the day
　　Comes and drags me from the hay,
　　That's the time
　　When I'm
　　In low.
He: Have you tried Pike's Peak, my dear
　　Kindly tell me, if so.
She: Yes, I've tried Pike's Peak, my dear,
　　But in the morning, no, no—no, no,
　　No, no, no, no, no!

REFRAIN 3

She: Are you fond of swimming, dear?
　　Kindly tell me, if so.
He: Yes, I'm fond of swimming, dear,
　　But in the morning, no.
She: Can you do the crawl, my dear?
　　Kindly tell me, if so.
He: I can do the crawl, my dear,
　　But in the morning, no.
　　When the sun through the blind
　　Starts to burn my poor behind
　　That's the time
　　When I'm
　　In low.
She: Do you use the breast stroke, dear?
　　Kindly tell me, if so.
He: Yes, I use the breast stroke, dear,
　　But in the morning, no, no—no, no,
　　No, no, no, no, no!

REFRAIN 4

He: Are you fond of Hot Springs, dear?
　　Kindly tell me, if so.
She: Yes, I'm fond of Hot Springs, dear,
　　But in the morning, no.
He: D'you like old Point Comfort, dear?
　　Kindly tell me, if so.
She: I like old Point Comfort, dear,
　　But in the morning, no.
　　When my maid toddles in
　　With my orange juice and gin,
　　That's the time
　　When I'm
　　In low.
He: Do you like Mi-ami, dear?
　　Kindly tell me, if so.
She: Yes, I like your-ami, dear,
　　But in the morning, no, no—no, no,
　　No, no, no, no, no!

NOTE: To satisfy the objections of some of the critics as well as the complaints of the Boston censors, Cole wrote the next two refrains:

REFRAIN 5

She: Are you good at football, dear?
　　Kindly tell me, if so.
He: Yes, I'm good at football, dear,
　　But in the morning, no.
She: Do you ever fumble, dear?
　　Kindly tell me, if so.
He: No, I never fumble, dear,
　　But in the morning, yes.
　　When I start with a frown
　　Reading Winchell upside down,
　　That's the time
　　When I'm
　　In low.
She: Do you like a scrimmage, dear?
　　Kindly tell me, if so.
He: Yes, I like a scrimmage, dear,
　　But in the morning, no, no—no, no,
　　No, no, no no, no!

REFRAIN 6

He: D'you like Nelson Eddy, dear?
　　Kindly tell me, if so.
She: I like Nelson Eddy, dear,
　　But in the morning, no.
He: D'you like Tommy Manville, dear?
　　Kindly tell me, if so.
She: I like Tommy Manville, dear,
　　But in the morning, no.
　　When my maid says, "Madame!
　　Wake 'em and make 'em scram,"
　　That's the time
　　When I'm
　　In low.
He: Are you fond of Harvard men?
　　Kindly tell me, if so.
She: Yes, I'm fond of Harvard men,
　　But in the morning, no, no—no, no,
　　No, no, no, no, no!

REFRAIN 7

She: Are you good at figures, dear?
　　Kindly tell me, if so.
He: Yes, I'm good at figures dear,
　　But in the morning, no.
She: D'you do double entry, dear?
　　Kindly tell me, if so.
He: I do double entry, dear,
　　But in the morning, no
　　When the sun on the rise
　　Shows the bags beneath my eyes.
　　That's the time
　　When I'm
　　In low.
She: Are you fond of business, dear?
　　Kindly tell me, if so.
He: Yes, I'm fond of business, dear,
　　But in the morning, no, no—no, no,
　　No, no, no, no, no!

REFRAIN 8

He: Are you in the market, dear?
　　Kindly tell me, if so.
She: Yes, I'm in the market, dear,
　　But in the morning, no.
He: Are you fond of bulls and bears?
　　Kindly tell me, if so.
She: Yes, I'm fond of bears and bulls,
　　But in the morning, no.
　　When I'm waked by my fat
　　Old canary, singing flat,
　　That's the time
　　When I'm
　　In low.
He: Would you ever sell your seat?
　　Kindly tell me, if so.
She: Yes, I'd gladly sell my seat,
　　But in the morning, no, no—no, no,
　　No, no, no, no, no!

REFRAIN 9

She: Are you fond of poker, dear?
　　Kindly tell me, if so.
He: Yes, I'm fond of poker, dear,
　　But in the morning, no.
She: Do you ante up, my dear?
　　Kindly tell me, if so.
He: Yes, I ante up-my dear,
　　But in the morning, no.
　　When my old Gunga Din
　　Brings the Bromo Seltzer in,
　　That's the time
　　When I'm
　　In low.
She: Can you fill an inside straight?
　　Kindly tell me, if so.
He: I've filled plenty inside straight,
　　But in the morning, no, no—no, no,
　　No, no, no, no, no!

REFRAIN 10

He: Are you fond of Democrats?
　　Kindly tell me, if so.
She: Yes, I'm fond of Democrats,
　　But in the morning, no.
He: Do you like Republicans?
　　Kindly tell me, if so.
She: Yes, I like Republi-cans,
　　But in the morning, no.
　　When my pet pekinese
　　Starts to cross his Q's and P's,
　　That's the time
　　When I'm
　　In low.
He: Do you like third parties, dear?
　　Kindly tell me, if so.
She: Yes, I love third parties, dear,
　　But in the morning, no, no—no, no,
　　No, no, no, no, no!

Bewitched
PAL JOEY
1940

Words by LORENZ HART
Music by RICHARD RODGERS

VERA:

He's a fool and don't I know it. But a fool can have his charms.

I'm in love and don't I show it, Like a babe in arms. Love's the same old

sad sen-sa-tion. Late-ly I've not slept a wink Since this half-pint im-i-ta-tion

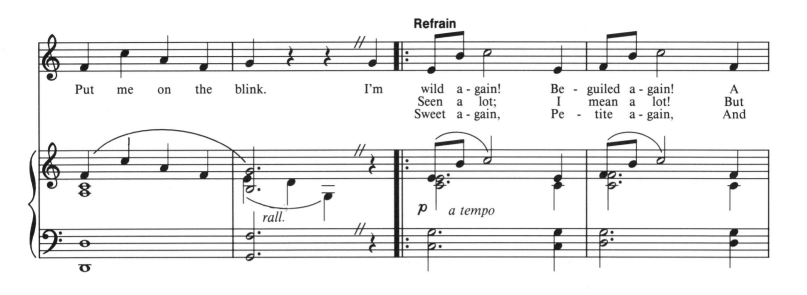

176

til I could sleep where I should-n't sleep. Be - witched, both-ered and be - wil - dered am
wor-ship the trou-sers that cling to him. Be - witched, both-ered and be - wil - dered am
think that he loves me, So hot am I. Be - witched, both-ered and be - wil - dered am

I._____ Lost my heart, but what of it?
I._____ When he talks He is seek - ing
I._____ Though at first we said "No, sir."

My mis - take, I a - gree. He's a laugh, but I love it___ Be - cause the
Words to get off his chest. Hor - i - zon - tal - ly speak - ing,___ He's at his
Now we're two lit- tle dears. You might say we are clos - er___ Than Roe - buck

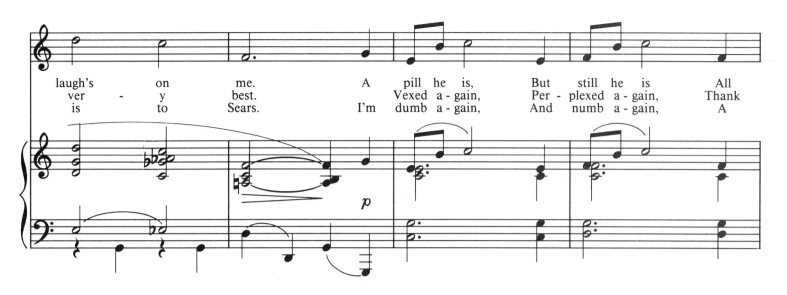

laugh's on me. A pill he is, But still he is All
ver - y best. Vexed a - gain, Per - plexed a - gain, Thank
is - to Sears. I'm dumb a - gain, And numb a - gain, A

p

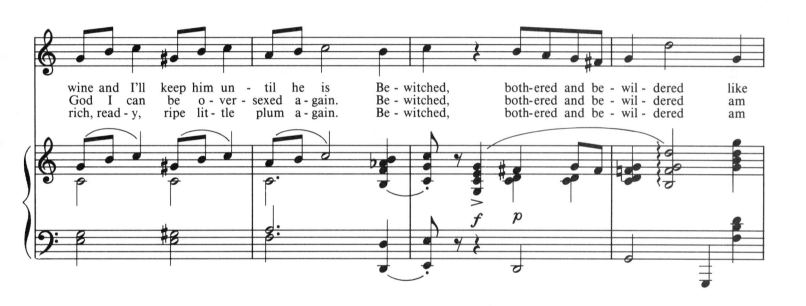

wine and I'll keep him un - til he is Be - witched, both-ered and be - wil - dered like
God I can be o - ver - sexed a - gain. Be - witched, both-ered and be - wil - dered am
rich, read - y, ripe lit - tle plum a - gain. Be - witched, both-ered and be - wil - dered am

f *p*

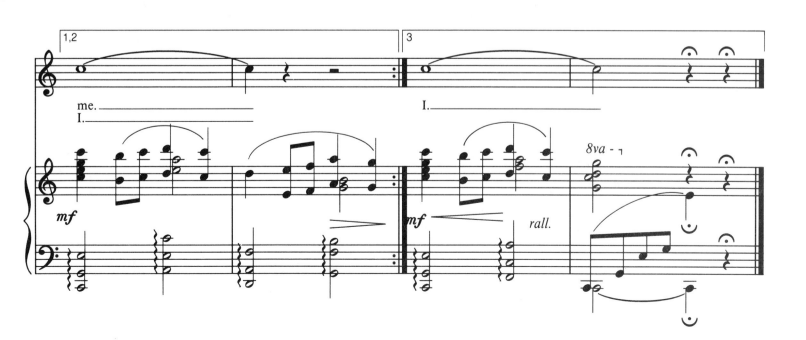

1,2
me.
I.
mf

3
I.
mf *rall.*
8va

My Ship
LADY IN THE DARK
1941

Words by IRA GERSHWIN
Music by KURT WEILL

WAIT TILL YOU SEE HER

BY JUPITER
1942

Words by LORENZ HART
Music by RICHARD RODGERS

Tempo di Valse

Wait till you see her, see how she looks, Wait till you

hear her laugh._____ Paint - ers of paint - ings,

writ - ers of books, Nev - er could tell the half._____

Wait till you feel the warmth of her glance,

OKLAHOMA

OKLAHOMA!
1943

Lyrics by OSCAR HAMMERSTEIN II
Music by RICHARD RODGERS

I Love You
MEXICAN HAYRIDE
1944

Words and Music by
COLE PORTER

If a love song I could on-ly write, ___ A song with words and mu-sic di - vine ___ I would ser - e - nade you ev - 'ry night ___ Till you'd re - lent and con-sent to be mine ___ But a-

190

You'll Never Walk Alone

CAROUSEL
1945

Lyrics by OSCAR HAMMERSTEIN II
Music by RICHARD RODGERS

Andantino molto cantabile

(with great warmth, like a hymn)

* alternate lyric: hold your head up high

195

There's No Business Like Show Business

ANNIE GET YOUR GUN
1946

Words and Music by
IRVING BERLIN

198

How Are Things in Glocca Morra
FINIAN'S RAINBOW
1947

Words by E.Y. HARBURG
Music by BURTON LANE

So in Love
KISS ME, KATE
1948

Words and Music by
COLE PORTER

There Is Nothin' Like a Dame

SOUTH PACIFIC
1949

Lyrics by OSCAR HAMMERSTEIN II
Music by RICHARD RODGERS

We got sun-light on the sand, We got moon-light on the sea, We got man-goes and ba-na-nas You can pick right off a tree, We got vol-ley ball and ping pong And a lot of dan-dy games! What ain't we got? We

We got nothin' to put on a clean white suit for. *What we need is what there ain't no substi - tute for.*
Lots of things in life are beautiful, but broth - er, *There is one particular thing that is nothin'*
whatsoever in any way, shape or form like any oth - er.

There is noth-in' like a dame, _____ Noth-in' in the

world, _____ There is noth-in' you can name That is

an - y - thin' like a dame! _____ We feel

If I Were a Bell
GUYS AND DOLLS
1950

By FRANK LOESSER

Medium Bounce

Ask me how do I feel___ Ask me now that we're co-sy and cling-ing___
how do I feel___ From this Chem-is-try les-son I'm learn-ing___

Well sir, all I can say___ is if I___ were a bell___ I'd be
Well sir, all I can say___ is if I___ were a bridge___ I'd be

ring-ing.___ From the mo-ment we kissed to-nite___
burn-ing.___ Yes, I knew my mor-ale would crack___

Shall We Dance?
THE KING AND I
1951

Lyrics by OSCAR HAMMERSTEIN II
Music by RICHARD RODGERS

Brightly (*moderato*)

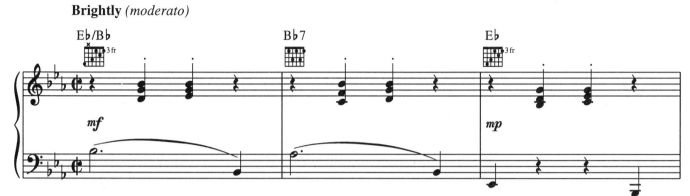

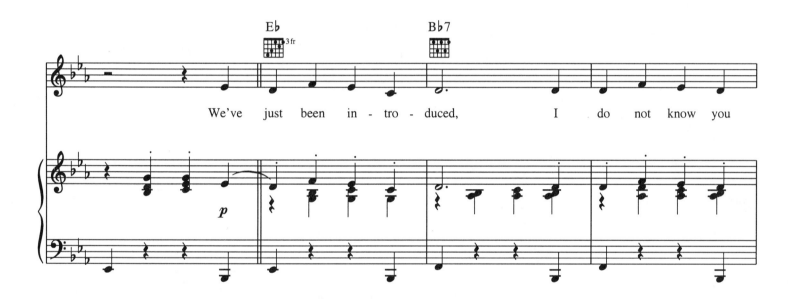

We've just been in - tro - duced, I do not know you

well. But when the mu - sic start - ed, some - thing drew me to your side. So

Wish You Were Here

WISH YOU WERE HERE
1952

Words and Music by
HAROLD ROME

Baubles, Bangles and Beads

KISMET
1953

Words and Music by ROBERT WRIGHT
and GEORGE FORREST
(Music Based on Themes of A. BORODIN)

Never Never Land
PETER PAN
1954

Lyric by BETTY COMDEN and ADOLPH GREEN
Music by JULE STYNE

PETER:

I know a place where dreams are born, and time is nev-er planned. It's not on an-y chart, you must

find it with your heart. Nev - er Nev - er Land. It might be miles be -

yond the moon or right there where you stand. Just keep an o - pen mind, and then

sud-den - ly you'll find Nev - er Nev - er Land. You'll have a trea-sure if you

stay there, more pre-cious far than gold. For once you have found your

All of You
SILK STOCKINGS
1955

Words and Music by
COLE PORTER

Fox Trot Tempo

With bounce, not too fast

Af - ter watch - ing her ap - peal from ev - 'ry an - gle, ____

____ There's a big ro - man - tic deal I've got to

wan - gle. ____ For I've fall - en for a

Wouldn't It Be Loverly
MY FAIR LADY
1956

Words by ALAN JAY LERNER
Music by FREDERICK LOEWE

SEVENTY-SIX TROMBONES
THE MUSIC MAN
1957

By MEREDITH WILLSON

Sev-en-ty six trom-bones led the big pa-rade,_____ with a hun-dred and ten cor-nets close at hand._____ They were fol-lowed by rows and rows of the

Love, Look Away
FLOWER DRUM SONG
1958

Lyrics by OSCAR HAMMERSTEIN II
Music by RICHARD RODGERS

Small World

GYPSY
1959

Words by STEPHEN SONDHEIM
Music by JULE STYNE

Make Someone Happy
DO RE MI
1960

Words by BETTY COMDEN and ADOLPH GREEN
Music by JULE STYNE

BROTHERHOOD OF MAN
HOW TO SUCCEED IN BUSINESS WITHOUT REALLY TRYING
1961

By FRANK LOESSER

Handclapping Spiritual Feel

What Kind of Fool Am I?
STOP THE WORLD—I WANT TO GET OFF
1962

Words and Music by LESLIE BRICUSSE
and ANTHONY NEWLEY

As Long as He Needs Me

OLIVER!
1963

Words and Music by
LIONEL BART

As long as he needs me — Oh yes he does need me — In spite of what you see — I'm sure that he needs me — Who else would love him still When they've been used so ill — He knows I al - ways will — As long as he needs me. I miss him so much — when he is

Tempo I

263

Don't Rain on My Parade

FUNNY GIRL
1964

Words by BOB MERRILL
Music by JULE STYNE

THE IMPOSSIBLE DREAM
(THE QUEST)
MAN OF LA MANCHA
1965

Lyric by JOE DARION
Music by MITCH LEIGH

1. To dream the im-pos-si-ble dream, to
(2. To) right the un-right-a-ble wrong, to

fight the un-beat-a-ble foe, To
love pure and chaste from a-far, To

bear with un-bear-a-ble sor-row, to
try when your arms are too wea-ry, to

MAME

MAME
1966

Music and Lyric by
JERRY HERMAN

Happiness
YOU'RE A GOOD MAN, CHARLIE BROWN
1967

Words and Music by
CLARK GESNER

I'll Never Fall in Love Again

PROMISES, PROMISES
1968

Lyric by HAL DAVID
Music by BURT BACHARACH

280

Love Song
CELEBRATION
1969

Words by TOM JONES
Music by HARVEY SCHMIDT

287

The Ladies Who Lunch
COMPANY
1970

Music and Lyrics by
STEPHEN SONDHEIM

Molto Rubato (♩ = 96)   JOANNE:

(Vocal sung 8vb) Here's to the la - dies who

lunch... Ev - 'ry - bod - y laugh.   Loung - ing in their

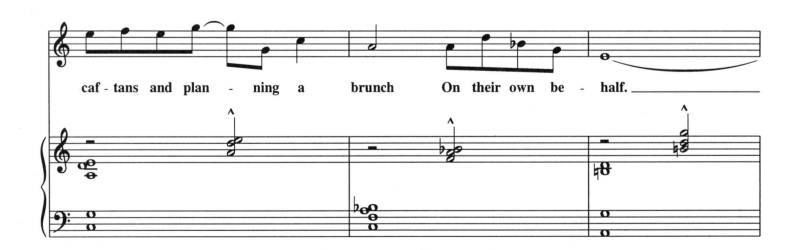

caf - tans and plan - ning a brunch   On their own be - half. _____

Off to the gym, Then to a fit - ting,

Claim - ing they're fat, _____ And look - ing grim

'Cause they've been sit - ting choos - ing a hat. __ *(Spoken:)Does anyone still wear a hat?*

rit.

Slow Bossa Nova (♩ = 108)

I'll drink to that.

p

Here's to the girls __ who stay smart. Are-n't they a gas?

Rush-ing to their class-es in op - ti-cal art, ___ Wish-ing it would

pass. An-oth-er long, ex-haust-ing day, __

An-oth-er thou - sand dol - lars. __ A mat - i - nee: A

here's to the girls _ who just watch, _ Are-n't they the best?

When they get de-pressed, it's a bot - tle of scotch, _ Plus a lit - tle

jest. An-oth-er chance to dis-ap - prove, _

An-oth-er bril - liant zin - ger. _____ An-oth-er rea - son

dies. _____ _

A toast to that in-vin-ci-ble bunch, _

_ The di-no-saurs sur-viv-ing the crunch, _ Let's

hear it for the la-dies who lunch: _ Ev-'ry-bod-y rise! _____

2 times

f

3 times

Rise! Rise! Rise! _____

cresc.

8vb

Day by Day
GODSPELL
1971

Words and Music by
STEPHEN SCHWARTZ

Beauty School Dropout
GREASE
1972

Lyric and Music by WARREN CASEY
and JIM JACOBS

Slow and Angelic

Your stor-y's sad to tell, a teen-age ne'er-do-well, most

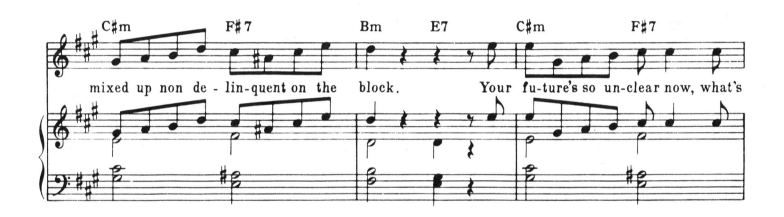

mixed up non de - lin-quent on the block. Your fu-ture's so un-clear now, what's

left of your ca-reer now, can't ev- en get a trade in on your smock.

D. % al Coda

CODA

pool, Turn in your teas-ing comb and go back to high school. Beau-ty School

sweat it,____ you're not cut out to hold a

job,____ Bet - ter for - get it,____ who wants their

hair done by a slob?____ Now, your bangs are curled, your

lash - es twirled, but still the world is cruel. Wipe off that

an - gel face and go back to high school.

Ya ooh.

Alice Blue Gown
IRENE (Revival)
1973

Lyric by JOSEPH McCARTHY
Music by HARRY TIERNEY

In my sweet lit-tle A-lice blue gown, _____ when I first wan-dered down in to town, _____ I was

305

I Won't Send Roses

MACK AND MABEL
1974

Music and Lyric by
JERRY HERMAN

Moderately

One
A CHORUS LINE
1975

Music by MARVIN HAMLISCH
Lyric by EDWARD KLEBAN

she is one of a kind.

Brighter Tempo

One sin - gu - lar sen - sa - tion

She walks in - to a room and you know she's un -

ev - 'ry lit - tle step she takes. com - mon - ly rare, ver - y u - nique, per - i - pa - tet - ic, po - et - ic and chic.

C7   F9   Bb7

real - ly have to men - tion, she's   the

her.   I'm a son __ of a gun, __ she is one __ of a

Ebmaj7   Fm7

one? _____

kind. _____

Ebmaj7   Fm7   **Repeat and Fade**

GOD BLESS' THE CHILD
BUBBLING BROWN SUGAR
1976

Words and Music by ARTHUR HERZOG JR.
and BILLIE HOLIDAY

Slowly with feeling

Them that's got shall get, Them that's not shall lose, So the

Bi - ble said, And it still is news; Ma-ma may have, Pa-pa may have, But

God bless the child that's got his own! That's got his own. Yes, the

Tomorrow
ANNIE
1977

Lyric by MARTIN CHARNIN
Music by CHARLES STROUSE

HONEYSUCKLE ROSE
AIN'T MISBEHAVIN'
1978

Words by ANDY RAZAF
Music by THOMAS "FATS" WALLER

Don't Cry for Me Argentina

EVITA
1979

Words by TIM RICE
Music by ANDREW LLOYD WEBBER

MCA Music Publishing

332

VERSE

prom‑ise, Don't keep your dis‑tance.____ 3. And as for

for‑tune and as for fame— I nev‑er in‑vi‑ted them in: Though it

seemed to the world they were all I de‑sired. They are il‑lu‑sions,— they're

not the so‑lu‑tions they prom‑ised to be, the an‑swer was here all the time____ I

The Best in the World

A DAY IN HOLLYWOOD/A NIGHT IN THE UKRAINE
1980

Music and Lyric by
JERRY HERMAN

D. S. al Coda 𝄉

1.2. B♭

3. B♭

best."
best.

2. Said good-bye to the   all.
3. I   was mold-ed and

4. Life can have its i-

Coda B♭maj7   G7-9   Cm   Cm7   F7

best! _____ I'm the best in the   world,

Cm7   F7   F7+5   B♭maj7   B♭6

I'm the best in the   world.

I'm the bright lit-tle

Any Dream Will Do

JOSEPH AND THE AMAZING TECHNICOLOR DREAMCOAT
1981

Music by ANDREW LLOYD WEBBER
Lyrics by TIM RICE

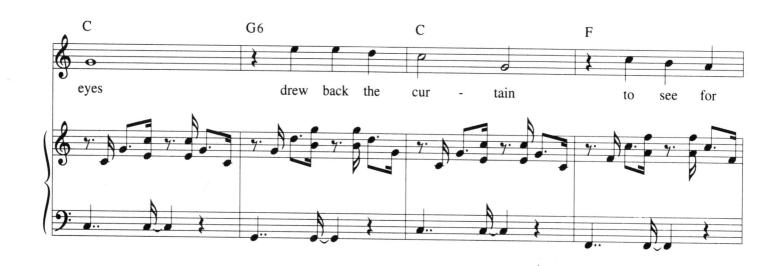

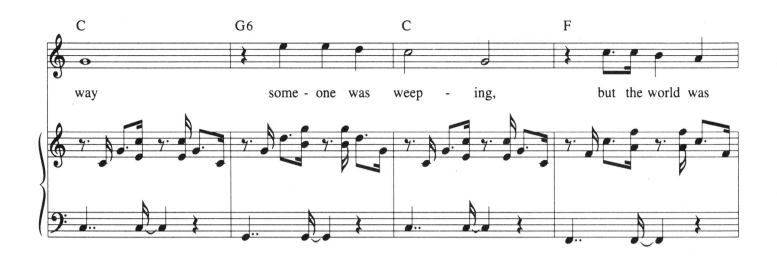

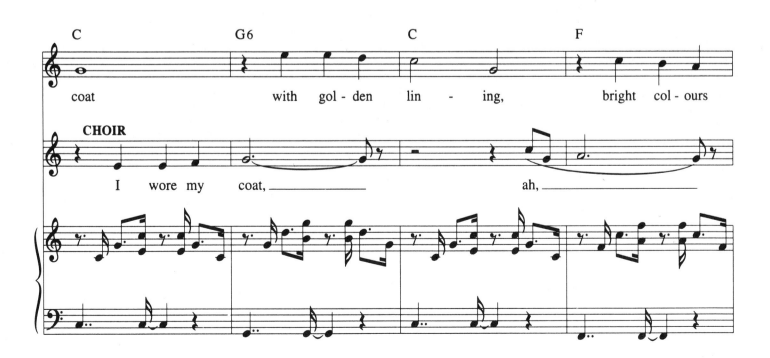

crash of drums _ a flash of light, _ my gold-en coat flew out of sight. _ The

CHOIR

The

col - ours fad - ed in - to dark - ness, I was left a - lone. _____

col - ours fad - ed in - to dark - ness, ah, _____ ah, _____

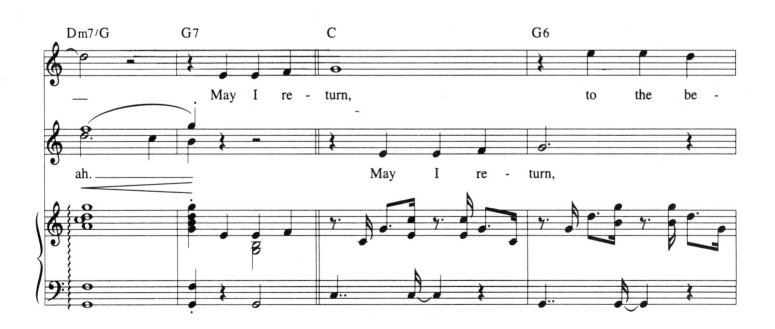

_ May I re - turn, to the be -

ah. _____ May I re - turn,

gin - ning, the light is dim - ming and the dream is
ah, _____ ah. _____

too, the world and I, we are still
The world and I, _____

wait - ing, still he - si - ta - ting a - ny dream will
ah, _____ ah. _____

Memory
CATS
1982

Music by ANDREW LLOYD WEBBER
Text by TREVOR NUNN after T.S. ELIOT

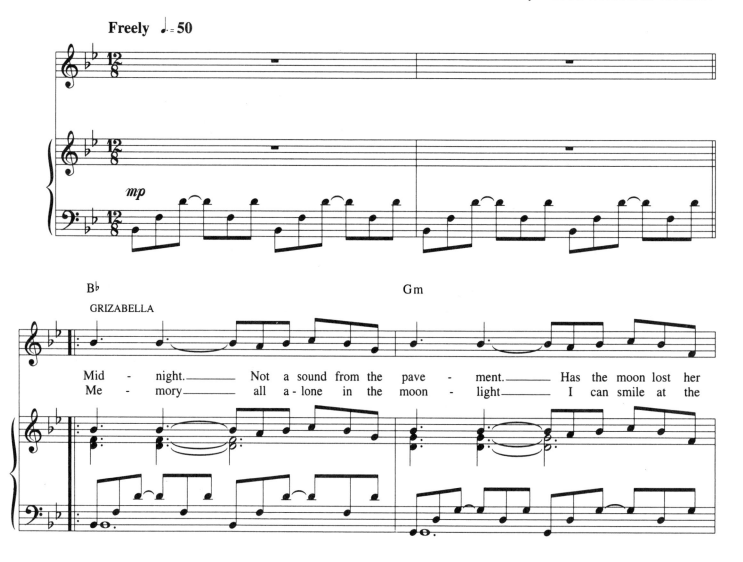

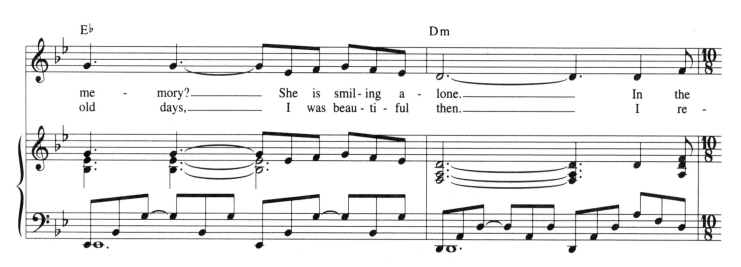

349

I Am What I Am
LA CAGE AUX FOLLES
1983

Music and Lyric by
JERRY HERMAN

Fabulous Feet
THE TAP DANCE KID
1984

Written by HENRY KRIEGER
and ROBERT LORICK

359

Tell Me on a Sunday
SONG & DANCE
1985

Music by ANDREW LLOYD WEBBER
Lyrics by DON BLACK

Don't write a let-ter when you want to leave,

don't call me at 3 a. m. from a friend's a-part-ment; I'd like to choose how I

366

Once You Lose Your Heart
ME AND MY GIRL
1986

Words and Music by
NOEL GAY

fol - low   your   heart.

They say a girl should nev - er be with -

out   love, _____   And   all   the   joy   that   love   a - lone   can

bring.   All   that   I   have   ev - er   learnt a -

bout   love, _____   Tells me   it's   a   ve - ry   fun - ny   thing.   For

372

I DREAMED A DREAM
LES MISÉRABLES
1987

Music by CLAUDE-MICHEL SCHÖNBERG
Lyrics by HERBERT KRETZMER
Original Text by ALAIN BOUBLIL and JEAN-MARC NATEL

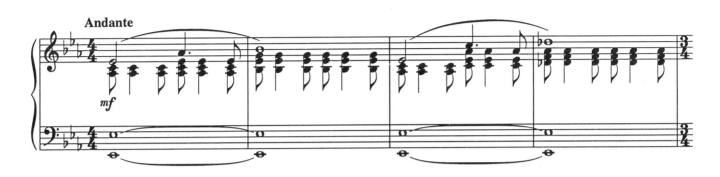

And the song was ex -cit -ing. There was a time. Then it all went wrong.

Andante

FANTINE:

I dreamed a dream in time gone by When hope was high and life worth liv -ing, I dreamed that love would nev - er die,

With their voi - ces soft as thun - der, As they tear your hope a -

part, As they turn your dream to shame.

rall. *a tempo*

He slept a sum - mer by my

side, He filled my days with end - less won - der,

He took my child-hood in his stride

But he was gone when au-tumn

poco accel.

came.

Più mosso 3

And still I dreamed he'd come to

cresc.

mf

(8vb ad lib.)

me.

That we would live the years to-geth-er.

But there are dreams that can-not be

And there are storms we can-not

weath-er.

I had a dream my life would

cresc. *f* *appassionato*

be

So dif-f'rent from this hell I'm liv - ing,_ So dif-f'rent now from what it

cresc.

poco rall. *a tempo*

seemed.

Now life has killed the dream I dreamed.

ff *dim.* *p*

rall.

All I Ask of You
THE PHANTOM OF THE OPERA
1988

Music by ANDREW LLOYD WEBBER
Lyrics by CHARLES HART
Additional Lyrics by RICHARD STILGOE

LOVE CAN'T HAPPEN
GRAND HOTEL
1989

Words and Music by
MAURY YESTON

Quickly, in one ♩. = 76

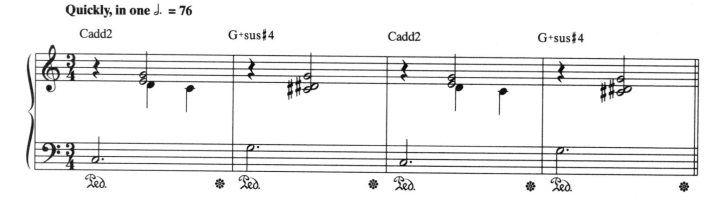

Ma - de - moi - selle, I have fol - lowed you ev - 'ry - where, al - most through-

sim.

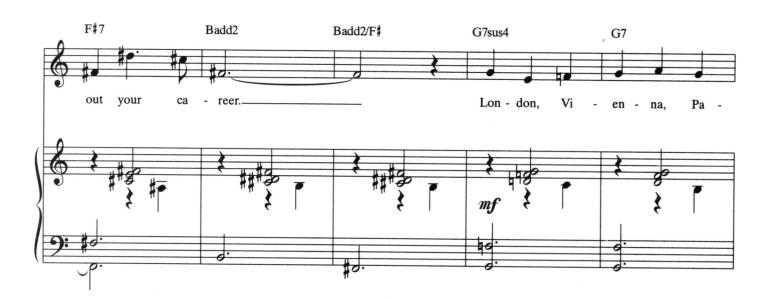

out your ca - reer._____ Lon - don, Vi - en - na, Pa -

mf

387

SEEING IS BELIEVING
ASPECTS OF LOVE
1990

Music by ANDREW LLOYD WEBBER
Lyrics by DON BLACK and CHARLES HART

ALEX: Seeing is believing, and in my arms I see her: she's
Seeing is believing. I dreamt that it would be her: at

here, really here, really mine now— she seems at home here...
last life is here, full, life is fine now...

What-ev-er hap-pens, one thing is cer-tain: each time I see a

THE LAST NIGHT OF THE WORLD
MISS SAIGON
1991

Music by CLAUDE-MICHEL SCHÖNBERG
Lyrics by RICHARD MALTBY JR. and ALAIN BOUBLIL
Adapted from original French Lyrics by ALAIN BOUBLIL

402

404

PLAY THE MUSIC FOR ME

JELLY'S LAST JAM
1992

Words by SUSAN BIRKENHEAD
Music by FERD "JELLY ROLL" MORTON

me.

Vocal ad lib.

double time feel

Jelly: **"Not Yet."**

Solo

When you're talk-in' you're talk-in' the mu - sic.

When you're walk-in' you're walk-in' the mu - sic.

Is You Is, or Is You Ain't

(Ma' Baby)
FIVE GUYS NAMED MOE
1993

Words and Music by BILLY AUSTIN
and LOUIS JORDAN

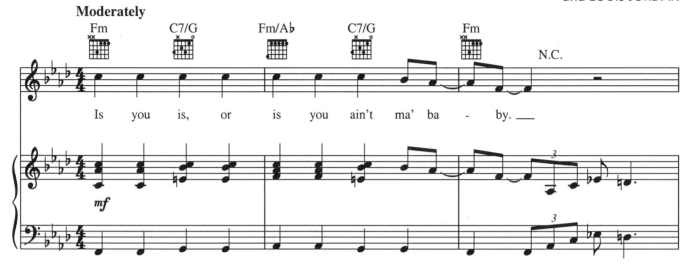

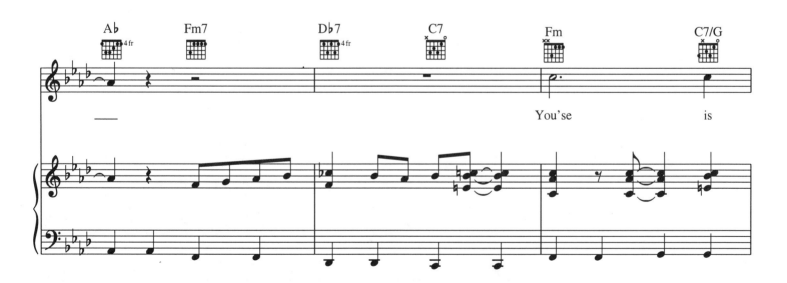

With One Look
Sunset Boulevard
1994

Music by ANDREW LLOYD WEBBER
Lyrics by DON BLACK and CHRISTOPHER HAMPTON,
with contributions by AMY POWERS

Living in the Shadows

VICTOR/VICTORIA
1995

Words by LESLIE BRICUSSE
Music by FRANK WILDHORN

Moderately slow

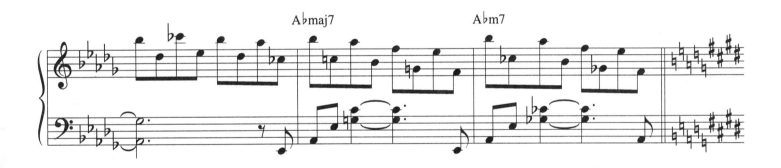

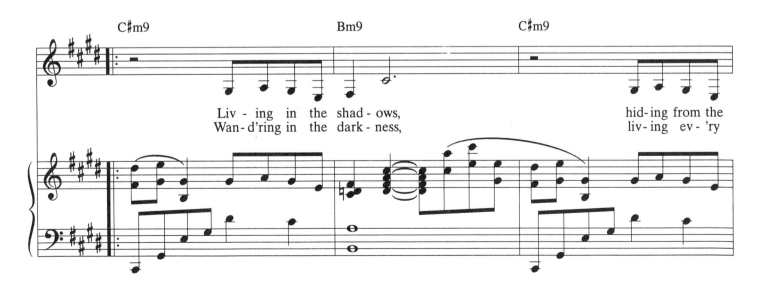

Liv - ing in the shad - ows,   hid-ing from the
Wan - d'ring in the dark - ness,   liv-ing ev - 'ry

Seasons of Love
RENT
1996

Words and Music by
JONATHAN LARSON

Circle of Life
THE LION KING: THE BROADWAY MUSICAL
1997

Music by ELTON JOHN
Lyrics by TIM RICE

Can You Find It in Your Heart?
FOOTLOOSE
1998

Words by DEAN PITCHFORD
Music by TOM SNOW

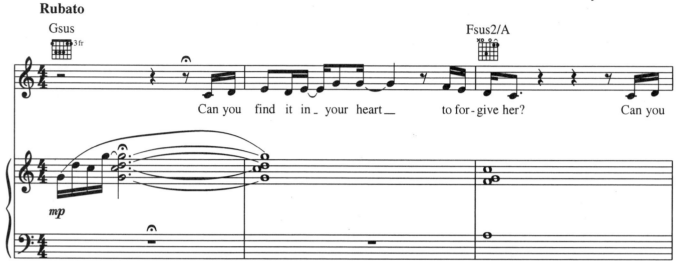

Can you find it in your heart __ to for-give her? __ Can you

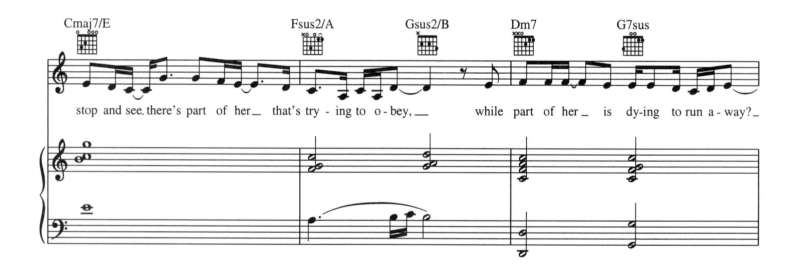

stop and see. there's part of her __ that's try-ing to o-bey, __ while part of her __ is dy-ing to run a-way? __

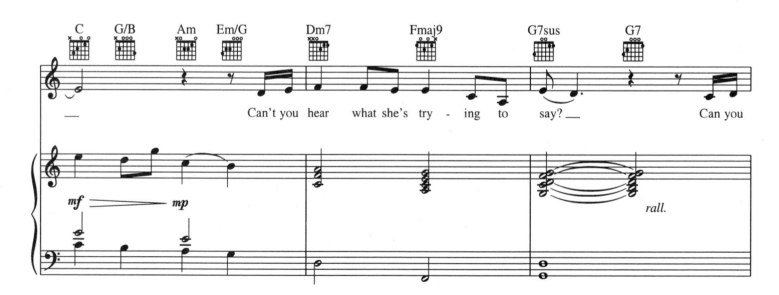

__ Can't you hear what she's try-ing to say? __ Can you

NIGHT FEVER
SATURDAY NIGHT FEVER
1999

Words and Music by BARRY GIBB,
MAURICE GIBB and ROBIN GIBB

BIG BOOKS OF MUSIC

Our "Big Books" feature big selections of popular titles under one cover, perfect for performing musicians, holiday sing-alongs, and music aficionados. All books are arranged for piano, voice, and guitar, and feature stay-open binding, so the books lie flat without breaking the spine.

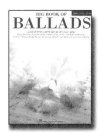
BIG BOOK OF BALLADS
63 SONGS.
00310485.........................$19.95

BIG BOOK OF CLASSICAL MUSIC
100 SONGS.
00310508.........................$19.95

BIG BOOK OF MOVIE MUSIC
72 SONGS.
00311582.........................$19.95

BIG BOOK OF BROADWAY
76 SONGS.
00311658.........................$19.95

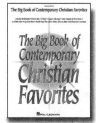
BIG BOOK OF CONTEMPORARY CHRISTIAN FAVORITES
50 SONGS.
00310021.........................$19.95

THE BIG BOOK OF NOSTALGIA
158 SONGS.
00310004.........................$19.95

BIG BOOK OF CHILDREN'S SONGS
55 SONGS.
00359261.........................$12.95

BIG BOOK OF COUNTRY MUSIC
64 SONGS.
00310188.........................$19.95

BIG BOOK OF RHYTHM & BLUES
67 SONGS.
00310169.........................$19.95

GREAT BIG BOOK OF CHILDREN'S SONGS
76 SONGS.
00310002.........................$14.95

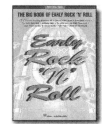
BIG BOOK OF EARLY ROCK N' ROLL
99 SONGS.
00310398.........................$19.95

BIG BOOK OF ROCK
78 SONGS.
00311566.........................$19.95

MIGHTY BIG BOOK OF CHILDREN'S SONGS
65 SONGS.
00310467.........................$14.95

BIG BOOK OF JAZZ
75 SONGS.
00311557.........................$19.95

BIG BOOK OF STANDARDS
86 SONGS.
00311667.........................$19.95

REALLY BIG BOOK OF CHILDREN'S SONGS
63 SONGS.
00310372.........................$15.95

BIG BOOK OF LATIN AMERICAN SONGS
89 SONGS.
00311562.........................$19.95

BIG BOOK OF SWING
84 SONGS.
00310359.........................$19.95

BIG BOOK OF CHRISTMAS SONGS
126 SONGS.
00311520.........................$19.95

BIG BOOK OF LOVE AND WEDDING SONGS
80 SONGS.
00311567.........................$19.95

BIG BOOK OF TV THEME SONGS
78 SONGS.
00310504.........................$19.95

FOR MORE INFORMATION, SEE YOUR LOCAL MUSIC DEALER,
OR WRITE TO:

Prices, contents, and availability subject to change without notice.

HAL•LEONARD®
CORPORATION
7777 W. BLUEMOUND RD. P.O. BOX 13819 MILWAUKEE, WI 53213

VISIT **halleonard.com** FOR OUR ENTIRE CATALOG
AND TO VIEW OUR COMPLETE SONGLISTS.

0699

BROADWAY'S BEST!

Broadway musicals have provided us with some of the most timeless and loved standards ever. This series highlights the show tunes that have kept us humming, dancing and crying for years! From classic shows like *A Chorus Line, Fiddler On The Roof* and *The Sound Of Music* to contemporary blockbusters such as *Phantom Of The Opera, Les Miserables,* and *Miss Saigon,* these books celebrate the Broadway tradition of unforgettable music. All books arranged for piano, voice and guitar.

BROADWAY BALLADS

Over 30 sentimental favorites from classic shows and contemporary blockbusters. Songs include: All I Ask Of You • Bewitched • I Dreamed A Dream • Memory • My Funny Valentine • On My Own • People • Send In The Clowns • September Song • Smoke Gets In Your Eyes • Sun And Moon • Unexpected Song • What I Did For Love • and many more.

00311570 ....$12.95

BROADWAY SHOWSTOPPERS

37 songs that bring the house down every time, including: Cabaret • Do You Hear The People Sing? • Don't Cry For Me Argentina • Everything's Coming Up Roses • Hello, Dolly! • I Am What I Am • Lambeth Walk • Memory • Oklahoma • and more.

00311629 ....$14.95

BROADWAY COMEDY SONGS

31 songs from the lighter side of Broadway, including: Dance: Ten, Looks: Three • I Want To Be Bad • I Wish I Were In Love Again • It's A Lovely Day For A Murder • A Little More Mascara • Sing Me A Song With Social Significance • Well, Did You Evah? • Your Feet's Too Big • and more.

00311630 ....$14.95

BROADWAY TORCH SONGS

This collection helps you sing your heart out with over 30 favorites from the stage, including: Can't Help Lovin' Dat Man • I Dreamed A Dream • I Loved You Once In Silence • The Party's Over • Send In The Clowns • Stormy Weather • Why Was I Born • and more.

00311628 ....$12.95

BROADWAY JAZZ

Over 30 Broadway hits that have become standard jazz repertoire, including: Ain't Misbehavin' • From This Moment On • How High The Moon • I Love Paris • It's De-Lovely • The Lady Is A Tramp • My Favorite Things • My Funny Valentine • Nice Work If You Can Get It • What Kind Of Fool Am I? • and many more.

00311569 ....$14.95

BROADWAY WALTZES

Over 40 songs that'll make you feel like dancing...from such shows as *Can-Can, Kiss Me, Kate, Sound Of Music, Les Miserables, La Cage Aux Folles, Phantom Of The Opera, South Pacific,* and more. Songs include: Allez-Vous-En, Go Away • Do I Hear A Waltz? • Edelweiss • Getting To Know You • Oh, What A Beautiful Mornin' • Sunrise, Sunset • Try To Remember • and many more.

00311568 ....$14.95

BROADWAY LOVE SONGS

Over 50 romantic favorites from shows such as *Phantom Of The Opera, Guys And Dolls, Aspects Of Love, Oklahoma!, South Pacific, Fiddler On The Roof,* and more. Songs include: All I Ask Of You • Bewitched • I've Grown Accustomed To Her Face • Love Changes Everything • So In Love • Sunrise, Sunset • Unexpected Song • We Kiss In A Shadow • and more.

00311558 ....$14.95

Prices, contents, and availability subject to change without notice. Some products may not be available outside the U.S.A.

For More Information, See Your Local Music Dealer, Or Write To:

HAL•LEONARD® CORPORATION

7777 W. Bluemound Rd. P.O. Box 13819 Milwaukee, WI 53213

0897